Who is more criminally responsible? :

The medicated person vs. the medicine maker

Mason Anthony Scott

© 12/22/14

Introduction

Ever Since man has walked the earth he has suffered physically, mentally and socially. Medicine men would offer help in a wide range of ways. For example, a treatment might be made from various herbs, sheep's dung, or other organic ingredient. There was even an operation called trephining which involved cutting open the head and letting the demon free.(New York Times) In each person was not so much a demon but different wiring, like fingerprints, no two brains are exactly alike. This makes each person unique in some way and often times they are too unique to the point that they do not fit in. This can sometimes make them a target for bullying.

Some of these treatments worked rather ingeniously. For instance, some Native American tribes brewed a special tea which would induce vomiting in the patient. However, different cultures offer different solutions, are unique and offer different philosophies where treatment options are concerned. And unfortunately, due to a society's lack of scientific knowledge and or religious beliefs, there were many more medical treatments which made the original problem(s) worse or even led to the patient's death. Bloodletting, an ancient practice of draining blood from people's bodies, was widespread and was a contributing factor to the death of George Washington.(Vadakan) People went on to commit acts that were either good or bad. It is the bad part that will be discussed in this paper and who is responsible for the bad part, the medicated person or the medicine maker.

No doubt most folks set out with good intentions; nobody sets out maliciously to harm their clients. But the modern world is ruled by the pursuit of money. This includes all aspects of business, including medicine and all aspects related to the field. The natural laws of economics tell us about the laws of supply and demand. Even the common street dealers know this. But money and profits can cloud judgment; or corrupt, and that is when people get hurt.

A host of problems occur when there is improper testing conducted by pharmaceutical companies or government agencies. Prescribing a drug beyond the recommended dose can lead to addiction or can compound a patient's already existing medical problems. In some cases, people that should not be taking the medications to begin with are given the medications by doctors who in turn receive reward for their efforts. Physicians can at times be held responsible also but it is always important to go back to the source, the pharmaceuticals companies themselves.

All of this does not completely exonerate the patient of responsibility for his or her actions. To a certain extent, free will should be taken into account. This is the right to choose- what we are free to do or not do- either the right thing or the wrong thing. But does a mentally disturbed person have the same free will or do they simply choose to ignore the consequences?

In defense of the medicine maker:

Prozac (or Fluoxetine) is an antidepressant that is sometimes used to treat depression, obsessive compulsive disorder and eating disorders.(nih) It was supposed to have helped a young man named Kip Kinkel from Oregon in 1998. He went on to kill his parents, two classmates and injure twenty two more. Afterwards Kip cried and claimed that he felt remorse for his actions. Kip though could have through his own conscious have stopped himself by remembering that if the rifle had been pointed his way and the bullet had hit him, it would have meant death. This is a part of free will, not only what will happen to you but how your actions may hurt others.

Eli Lilly has won seventy lawsuits against them from people claiming that the drug Prozac made them do bizarre things. Surely 70 sets of jurors could see something that the rest of us don't want to see, that sometimes people are just wired differently and will commit crimes no matter what happens. Perhaps it was not something physically wrong with Kip but it was more social, he hated standing out, as do most people but Kip was a loner and there is no cure for being socially awkward or learning disabled. It is entirely possible that Kip would have contemplated these acts even if he were not on medication due to social pressures to fit in.

On May 20, 1998 Kip decided that if he was not to be accepted then he must turn against those that did not accept him. Was this Eli Lilly's fault? Kip discontinued his use of Prozac in the fall of 1997 but went on his killing spree in May of 1998. Before that his therapist reported him as being fine and making progress. When one adds a nail to keep wood together, is it wise then to remove the nail? No, the Prozac served a purpose, it kept Kip together.

In defense of drug makers, there is only so much that they can do. They cannot make some one more socially acceptable, they cannot cure the learning disabled and they cannot stop over indulgent parents. They can however help someone chemically; this in turn helps them with their social awkwardness which in turn makes them less of a target. All the individual has do is stay on the medication.

Pfizer alone spends 7 billion dollars a year on research and development of their products.(Mital) Some of the products that they produce and test do not make it past the in house approval list. The ones that do then may spend years languishing at the Food and Drug Administration awaiting approval.

Time is money and the sooner the drug is approved the faster the pharmaceutical company can make a return on their money. Some corners may be cut and approval may be rushed in the name of money and profit. If the system were based on being marketed toward one type of person, the process may go faster but the drug company wants to treat as many different kinds of ailments as possible, the more people that are treated the more money that can be made.

This is where people like Kip are caught in the mix, he was one of the many different ailments that could be treated, but he may have been too young for such a strong medication. A boy so young had a learning disability that was more of a social problem then a medical one. It was being different that made Kip depressed and the only cure for that is acceptance and understanding.

The doctor that treated Kip should have seen this and focused on that but instead he knew that the mother and Kip wanted quick results and also he knew that he had incentives to prescribe the medication from the pharmaceutical company. But if this were the case and each person had an interest in helping Kip whether it were parentally or financially then they should have made sure that he stayed on the medication no matter what. But they let him lapse because they believed he was better, they couldn't have been more wrong.

It was after this that Kip had an episode that ended in murder. There was plenty of blame to go around but some of it should be placed at the feet of the adults and guardians that were supposed to protect Kip from himself. Barring the negative side effects medicines can produce, it is important to remember that a physician should be consulted with before a medication is suddenly stopped and parents need to here and answer about the consequences of such an action.

The devil made me do it:

In the modern world people suffer the same mental issues as they did a thousand years ago. Some things never change though, wars that bring people home the mentally affected for life, genes that were passed down through the ages from parent to child and everyday normal stresses such as work, family and friends. It is a never ending cycle with no cure in sight, especially on a planet with six billion different people and six billion different minds.

The only thing that has changed is the availability of drugs that are meant to soothe but not cure. The medications are designed to balance a person's mood. If balanced means being indifferent, that would be ideal but some people swing too far one way and then another. And even some pharmaceutical companies would have people that they are depressed when they are not.

Being indifferent can make the person worse though. They do not care one way or the other, they are not happy about what they are doing but they are not sad about it either. They do it because it feels like the thing to do at that moment, this is poor impulse control. Some of these people are normal everyday sociopaths, a person that is bent on doing what feels good to them and the consequences be damned.

These are people on that get a charge from doing negative things. It is the rush of adrenaline that fuels the desire to commit crimes or acts of violence. In order to maintain the rush, they must either keep doing negative things or worse things. There is no need for medications for this type of person, they are who they are and do not wish to change.

Some though are born this way and have no choice in their behavior; they are affected by issues such as ADHD, anxiety disorder, depression and other mood disorders.

These people can be given drugs but may still go on to commit crimes. If they are medicated, what makes them still commit crimes and violence against others? Is it free will?

Once again let us look at free will. Some people will drink and abuse drugs no matter how many pills they are given. They either lack the self-control over their will or they cannot stand not having that the rush that comes from doing something negative. They became accustomed to the feeling of being high and out of control.

My Position

It is never a good idea to put profits before people. And it is never a good idea to confuse physical issues with social issues. Plus some people will never change no matter what is done for them, they prefer problems over peace.

The pharmaceuticals want to make money, so they look for issues that people have and attempt to find a solution. Even if the person does not have an issue, they can persuade the general public with commercials based on generalities that they do. This is business, nothing more nothing less. They are there to make money.

Some people though have issues that are beyond their control. They are born with a brain that causes them to think and act different from others. The medications work for them so long as they stay on them. But just as their awkwardness brought unwelcome attention the medications bring stigma. They do not want to be different even if means being unstable.

Then are some people whether they medicated or not that will commit negative acts. They prefer life this way. There is only cure for them, being socially isolated in an institution that can keep them from harming themselves or others.

The people have only themselves to blame, not the pharmaceuticals. The pharmaceuticals only reacting to a market need. It is the people that keep it going. Much like the drug dealers, if they didn't have a market, they wouldn't deal drugs.

The Experiment

My experiment would be to find to people same age, sex, and criminal back ground that have a mental issue. A case manager would monitor their behavior and a psychiatrist would evaluate them physically.

Each would be given the same opportunity such as a job and a place to live. They would then be monitored and report to the case manager weekly for a year. One of the men would be given medication and the other wouldn't.

The psychiatrist would evaluate them monthly to check their minds and bodies at the same time. If thought one showed signs of anxiety or the potential to commit a crime the experiment would be ended and the

participant would be given full mental help.

References

N/A (2010).*Proofs of Ancient Surgery: Skulls Were Trephined to Allow Demons to Escape.* New York Times. Retrieved from query.nytimes.com/gst/abstract.html

Mital, Tushar (2009) Pfizer. Know the Co. Retrieved from www.knowtheco.com/index.php?news=23

Vadakan,V ibul V.Dr. (2002) *The Asphyxiating and Exsanguinating Death of President George Washington.* Presented at the Annual Miranda Lecture Series of Kaiser Permanente Bakersfield 2002 . Retrieved from xnet.kp.org/permanentejournal/spring04/time.html

N/A (2010). *Fluoxetine (Prozac).* NCBI. Retrieved from www.nlm.nih.gov

Abraham Maslow

The Genius

The Early Years

Mason Anthony Scott

© 12/22/14

The Early Years

Abraham Maslow started out life the hard way, born as the first child of seven in to a family that was already crashing in upon themselves before he came along. His parents were poor Jewish Russian immigrants that were caught in a loveless marriage. A perfect dysfunctional family of the early twentieth century born a man that would define what made people happy.

He described his mother as "a horrible creature" (Schultz) and his father was a womanizing drunk that would abandon the family (Schultz). The is typical of a very dysfunctional family, the mother could be described as an enabler for allowing the father to even have the slightest contact with her children, but alas the 1900's were a different time for a woman with no social support system she had no other choice but to allow him to keep contact with the family, if nothing else it made the house seem like a home.

Maslow did not let this keep him down. During the first half of the twentieth century there was no internet or television to distract him or electronically soothe the pain of a terrible home life. The local library became his sanctuary, a home away from that kept his spirits up. Not all people are meant to for sports; some are here for their intellect. Here Maslow was already showing his strengths.

Maslow began as a behaviorist (Schultz) inspired by John Watson, known for his "little Albert" experiment. Watson would give a child a harmless white rat and every time the child held it, Watson would make the loud noise that would frighten the child; this became the basis for an unconditioned stimulus response. The child then associated the white rat with loud noise and began to fear the white rat and at the sight of it, he would begin to cry because he had associated the white rat with the loud that was sure to follow.

Later he met Max Wertheimer, a Gestalt psychologist (Schultz); Gestalt is "a system of psychology that focuses largely on learning and perception." (Schultz) A system of psychology that looks at the whole rather than the pieces, it could be compared to the modern day bio psychosocial method that into account a person's physical, mental and social support system that allows a social worker or psychologist to make a more informed decision for the treatment.

Out of the depths of his personal sadness that Maslow was sure to affect many people though came from his inspiration. Abraham Maslow grew up to be responsible for one of the greatest psychological theories of the twentieth century. Oddly enough it was his mother and his dysfunctional family that inspired his theories, the one group of people who made him the most miserable.

Hierarchy of Needs

Maslow believed that in order for a person to be happy that they must satisfy five needs, physiological needs, safety needs, kinship, self-esteem and need for self-actualization. Each one of the needs, the lower first must be met before self-actualization can happen and true happiness can be found. Although this sounds difficult it is possible if one is willing to let go of some material needs.

Physiological needs are food, water and sex. Food and water are basic to human biology, meaning that they are needed in order to keep the body functioning and healthy. But sex is the weakest of these needs; it is not likely that anyone ever died from the lack of the act. Sex is a gratifying experience that satisfies the soul but is also something that was originally intended for reproduction purposes only.

Safety needs are security, order and stability. Security is the need to feel safe in our homes and our lives. Order is composed of some type of structure that insures that things happen in an order. Stability is knowing that someone is making sure that all these things are happening, a leader. Different people fulfill these needs for us, such as the policeman, civil service employees and elected officials. It is to be noted though we hope that these people have obtained some level of self-actualization so that they can be happy making us feel secure. This level seems to go hand in hand.

Kinship needs are friends and love. Friends are the people that help accentuate all the lower two needs. For example a partner that enjoys sex and other interest. Love is what we need from the friends; it says that I am here for you no matter what. Friends are there when you a person loses their source of income and provide a helping until the person can support themselves.

Self-esteem needs are acknowledgement for our actions that build self-worth. It is important to know that our lives meant something. Friends and colleagues are the only people we expect to give this to us. They show their appreciation or adoration for us by showing faith in us by appointing us to levels of responsibility or presenting us with awards that adorn our walls, a reminder of achievement and our next in self-actualization.

Self-actualization is "The highest level is self-actualization, or the self-fulfillment. Behavior in this case is not driven or motivated by deficiencies but rather one's desire for personal growth and the need to become all the things that a person is capable of becoming." (Learning-Theories.com) At this point a person of age should have reached a high level self-actualization. Food and water are still necessary but sex is an afterthought. Safety and security is achieved by selecting and moving into a neighborhood that has a high level of protection provided by a well-funded police department and/or private security guards. Kinships have been achieved through various social groups or organizations that are committed to a single goal. Self-esteem has been achieved but is beginning to be maxed out due to time and repeated offerings of appreciation, any other words it has meaning but the meaning diminishes

People are basically survivalist at heart; this has been instilled in them since the time of the great exodus from Africa. Their first priority was to survive in a land that one was either the eater or the eaten. If they had time and the conditions were right, reproduction was a priority. Of course there was safety in numbers, so naturally people banded together to improve their odds of survival. The highest self-esteem was to be named the leader, this honor said, "We believe in you and feel that you are the best person to help us survive." Naturally anyone who wanted this title would have strove for through actions. Anyone who didn't would have stayed in the back of the pack

Maslow's Influence on culture

Maslow could have had some influence on the hippie movement of the sixties in a counterproductive way. In other words they may have used it to justify their lifestyle of open and free sex and a fight against the system mentality. This an example of another person works being used to exploit a lifestyle and seek acceptance for that lifestyle.

For example the first of the pyramid of self-actualization, physiological needs. During the sixties there was a sexual revolution that encouraged experimentation beyond the boundaries of normal society. It is necessary for society to be open to change and this in turn grants everyone the chance to be happy and reach self-actualization. Different people need different things to make them happy. The sexual revolution or free love meant that you could experiment outside of the norms; a person could have multiple partners for example. But this

Need for this type of sex may not have been what Maslow was talking about. One person could have one partner for life and be just as happy. But there will always be the one group who need more or to take anything to the extreme.

The hippie movement was about going against the established system, for example fighting the system that provided order and stability. During the 1960's police officers and other symbols that are known to protect and serve were seen as authoritarian. These are people that lay down their lives to protect us but to the hippie movement they were seen as part of the problem, a barrier to freedom. The hippie movement was part of a struggle freedom to live a life outside of normal and established boundaries that brought the hippies themselves self-actualization.

Kinship may have been the start of the commune part of the hippie movement. People that are lost will often ban together for mutual support. But then again people living in a neighborhood and leading separate lives could accomplish the same thing. Communes though became an extension of the lifestyle that promoted a life outside the norm. The only difference was that it was more interconnected, a place where food and security depended more of a mutual benefit system. Whereas in normal society a person is paid a salary to provide the service and that person is subject to being replaced.

Self-esteem in the hippie movement was about loving yourself first and others would accept a person as they were. Hippies considered whatever you did for the group as positive; giving rather than taking was more likely to elevate that person to a higher position within the group. The more a person did for the group the positive it felt and the more positive a person feels, the more that person can love themselves and be inclined to do.

Self-actualization in the hippie movement may have been counter to what Maslow envisioned but the ground work was there. The hippie movement took what he wrote and used to remake society in their eyes. And in every social experiment there are good and bad elements. It did open the door to promiscuous sex but certain boundaries to a person's happiness had been torn down. For example homosexuality and interracial love was allowed to flourish and bring people happiness with the one they truly loved.

Robert Maslow Industrial Contribution

At the time Maslow was being born, women were pushing for equality in politics and economics. Machines were doing more manual labor and life on the farm was becoming a thing of the past. The mind of every person was expanding and new thoughts were gaining ground.

The average man lived to 47 years old and women lived to be 46.Social unrest saw the rise of the unions and women's suffrage organized their first parade. In a sense the general public was seeking self-actualization.

For example it was discovered that 20 percent of American children were malnourished and the middle class was unhappy. It was a time of unrest that began a social change. People were stretching their faculties to the limit.

It was found through Maslow's work in Hierarchy of Needs, that people have "different needs and therefore need to be motivated by different incentives to achieve organizational

objectives."(www.enotes.com > Encyclopedia of Small Business) and that

as one person reached a new point on the Hierarchy of Needs that person

needs then changed. This changed incentives in the work place from

monetary based system to a needs based system, hence health care and

decent working conditions.

Wundt and Maslow

Night and Day

Wilhelm Wundt (1832-1920), was the founding father, although

not originator of modern psychology. "He established the first laboratory,

edited the first journal, and began experimental psychology as a science."

(Schultz, p.90) Wundt was a German gentleman who originally intended

to become a physician, but it was while attending the university, that he

soon realized his true academic strengths lied in physiology and research.

In particular, Wundt was interested in founding psychology, which up to

that time was not a formal science. Because of his background in

research, he recognized that in order to legitimize psychology, he would

have to use physiology and research. He turned his attention to things like sensation and perception and reaction and association. Wundt wrote books publishing his experiments about psychology, worked from a lab, which he started in his own home and eventually in 1867, taught the first ever course about psychology at Heidelberg University.

Wundt was a prodigious writer, and it has been shown that between 1853 and 1920, he wrote 54,000 pages! His knowledge drew students from around the world. At the height of his popularity, his courses drew more than 600 students. Wundt envisioned the creation of what he called social psychology, and he was also interested in what today's terms would be called consciousness. Given that today's technical and medical knowledge is far better than it was in Wundt's own time, it is not surprising that some of his opinions and ideas have since been discredited or expanded upon. What is more important however, is the fact that Wundt was first to do so and that in itself makes him a pioneer and puts him in a prestigious place in psychology.

Twice, Wundt was nominated for a Nobel Prize. Unfortunately, his private political views about World War I made him unpopular with the English and Americans. He was unabashedly, pro German and his views tied in with strong Anti-German sentiment at the time. Gestalt psychology, psychoanalysis, functionalism and behaviorism all came into vogue at the time and Wundt lost favor. His achievements are nonetheless important.

But there were those that questioned Wundt's work, particularly "his method of introspection." (Shultz) Other researchers asked how one measure the correct response of the participants could if each one was different and no one could recreate the same response from another person. This is part of a peer review; the experiment must be done so as to be repeatable.

With Maslow and his Hierarchy of Needs it would be possible to repeat his work. For example, anyone without food or water will not skip this step and go to straight to worry about their safety. Their first thought would be to find something to eat or drink; some would even commit crimes to obtain these needs.

Whereas Wundt was in favor of one country invading another, Maslow may have helped to inadvertently end a war. The hippie movements' twisted adaptation of Maslow's work started a movement to end the Vietnam War.

Oddly enough after world war I it may have there may have been a twist of both Maslow and Wundt's work, Maslow's Hierarchy of Needs was in place in war ravaged Germany, a country of starving people and Wundt's introspection was needed by a country that had started a terrible war.

The sad part is that the man who became their conscious or introspection was one of the most hate filled men that ever lived.

Where it all began

Academically Maslow began at the City College of New York, in order to please his parents he studied law. But after three semesters he transferred to Cornell and then transferred back to City College of New York. (Boeree)

At this time he also married Bertha Goodman, his first cousin. After receiving his doctorate from the University of Wisconsin he returned to New York where he began teaching at Brooklyn College.

From 1951 to 1969 he served as the chair of psychology at Brandeis University. It is there that he met Kurt Goldstein, author of "The Organism", and the idea of self-actualization came to him. The Organism by Goldstein states that, "The organism cannot be divided into "organs" and far less into "mind" and "body", because it is the whole that reacts to the environment. Nothing is independent within the organism. The organism is a whole."(Piero Scaruffi).

Maslow discovered that in order to be truly happy, the whole person's needs must be taken into consideration. What he discovered in working with monkeys is that some needs are more important than others and that there is a possible deficit in needs or D-needs. (Boeree) If you are lacking a key element in your life, you will not be satisfied until you get. For example if a body is lacking energy and an orange comes to mind, it is something the body needs.

Even love is needed and it is an instinct or as Maslow called it,"an instinctoid", a built in need. (Boeree) For example a child that lacks love at birth faces may face emotional needs and are "grossly delayed in motor and mental development."(whyfiles.org/087mother/4.html)

Dr. Boeree goes on to talk about Maslow's "Philosophy of the Future"; simply you ask people what they need to make them happy. If one is hungry, a way would be made to feed them, this cutting down on their "Fixation" and allowing them to make a leap towards the next step in self-actualization. This is one of the reasons social programs are so important, they help the needy and get them to that next level. Plus it helps to cut down on crime and allows a person to go on with their life.

Maslow believed that once a person reached self-actualization there is a need to do more to fulfill self-actualization. To be more than you already are and return the fruits of good fortune to others and help them in turn realize self-actualization. (Boeree) The only point then is to grow spiritually; this in turn leads to charity, such as Bill Gates, a person that has reached self-actualization. He in turn helps others to achieve their self-actualization with charities that fight hunger, disease and illiteracy.

According to Dr. Boeree, Maslow used a method called biographical analysis to study such people. Maslow picked people from history and studied them to see how they self-actualized and what "characteristics they possessed." (Boeree) He found that these successful people were "reality centered"; they knew when something was real or fake. (Boeree)

They had "something Maslow called democratic values, meaning that they were open to ethnic and individual variety, even treasuring it."

(Boeree) This is most important in the kinship part of self-actualization; different people from different backgrounds bring something unique to a friendship

Each quality brings something out of the person causing the friend to grow and expand their mind and understanding. All of this was based on something Maslow called human kinship, "social interest, compassion and humanity." (Boeree) People want to get along, they want to live in a world where they can laugh and love.

Maslow was never under the impression that people were perfect, in fact some of the people that had reached self-actualization were guilt ridden and anxious, but there guilt and anxiety was not misplaced. They also "were absent minded and overly kind" (Boeree), some could even be cold and humorless.

This is possibly one of the drawbacks to self-actualization; it is hard to achieve all that there is without sacrificing something of one's self. Some people must lose out if all needs met. The people of the amazon have lost millions of acres so that cattle can be fed on grazing grounds.

For a home to provide safety and security people must be hired to provide that comfort but some of those people die in the process of providing that part of self-actualization. It goes even deeper than that, some people sacrifice friendships and loves in order to achieve the next level of self-actualization.

Conclusion

Every person on earth has purpose, in one way or another we are for each other. Most people are basically kind and just want to live and get along, being happy knowing that they are safe and well fed. Some people though are not that fortunate and must be suffer the lowest feelings in life. Maslow's life started out horribly but he did not let that stop him achieving. He found a sanctuary that served as a home, the library gave him the feeling of being safe that the never felt at home. Later in his life he found kinship in a family and friends who made him the chair of psychology at Brandeis and gave him the self-esteem he never had as a child. He reached his self-actualization; he had taken a terrible time in his life and made it in to something that made everybody's life better.

Reference Page

Boeree, George C. Dr. (2008).*Personality Theories.* Abraham Maslow

1908-1970. Retrieved from webspace.ship.edu/cgboer/maslow.html

Scaruffi,Piero (2000). *Kurt Goldstein: The Organism: A Holistic Approach to*

Biology (American Book 1939) Retrieved from

www.scaruffi.com/mind/goldstei.html

Schultz,Duane P. and Schultz, Ellen(2008). *A History of Modern*

Psychology. Wadsworth. Belmont, CA.

N/A (2008). Maslow's Hierarchy of Needs. Retrieved from www.learning-

theories.com/maslow-hierarchy-of-needs

N/A (1999). *The Science of a Mothers Day*. University of Wisconsin.

Retrieved from whyfiles.org/087mother/4.html

Critical Thinking and My Future

Mason Anthony Scott

© 12/22/14

"You must be single minded. Drive for the one thing on which you have decided". George S. Patton, Jr. (1885 - 1945), four star Army General. I believe a person can most certainly have more than one goal.

My decision making-process is based upon my lifelong need to improve myself and rise above my upbringing and family history. The critical thinking process I employed as a youth relied on looking at where I was and where I needed to be. I was lost in my youth, I had nobody to inspire me and push me. Everyone was content in writing me off. My mind was always racing over the possibilities. So much so that I was tested for autism at one point. Luckily, in my later years, there were people who saw potential in me and cared enough to encourage me to excel.

I primarily grew up in a rural setting much like my parents. They were content in experiencing life with a basically literacy level and had no desire to go beyond their comfort zone of limited knowledge. On the other hand, I was always the one in the family to question everything I heard and to break it down to a finite understanding. For example, on Sundays at church I would listen attentively and afterwards question the sermon scientifically, socially, and philosophically. I was often branded a pseudo heretic for asking questions and challenging beliefs. Paul and Elder (2001) stated it best, "Recognize that you are seeking a new way to look at learning. Recognize that it will take time to become comfortable in this new perspective. Consider your task as a student to be to learn new ways to think. Stretching the mind to accommodate new ideas is crucial" (Part I, p. 14).

I wanted more knowledge and would often ask deep thinking questions and in the interim managed to exhaust the Mississippi school system librarians as they tried to reference and find the sources to answer to my questions. One question inevitably led to more questions. I had no idea at the time that I was in actuality using the steps to becoming a critical thinker. Ridding oneself of biases and assumptions, looking for connections in ideas, and asking questions are part of the equation of becoming a great thinker.

I came from a long line of nefarious people so naturally I researched criminology as my first choice in careers, but law enforcement is mostly dedicated to punishment, rather than analysis, which has been always a source of fascination. I am interested in the prevention of the incident or at least finding solutions that may predict future behavior. According to Kurland (2000), "Critical thinkers are by nature skeptical. They approach texts with the same skepticism and suspicion as they approach spoken remarks. Critical thinkers are active, not passive. They ask questions and analyze. They consciously apply tactics and strategies to uncover meaning or assure their understanding.

I asked different professors what was the one field that would settle my natural curiosity about people and they informed me that psychology looks to the root cause of human actions and behaviors. I talked to a few psychologists about what made them opt for their chosen field and what was involved in becoming a psychologist. They explained to me that it was a need to make a difference in the lives of others and to help them end or at the least soften their psychological suffering.

I looked at many sub-fields and asked myself the question, "What am I capable of and what do I love to do?" I chose educational psychology because during my time in the military I planned, prepared, and led many classes, which I taught methodically and informatively. Personally, it gave me a feeling of pride and raised my self-esteem when soldiers who could perform their duties more efficiently.

The military was furtive ground for leadership. One must have confidence in the decision making process. The military was also my first exposure away from my southern roots and I found myself exposed to peoples of all backgrounds for the first time in my life. Diversity or rather the openness to it fosters personal growth. To be a critical thinker, one must essentially see the problem from all angles. I walked away from a career in the military knowing that I wanted a profession that would serve two purposes: one, to help others and two, to search for solutions to problems.

This is why I want to be a teacher and a psychologist, not just any teacher though but a teacher who is challenged daily and can make the greatest of contributions. I have chosen to specialize in educating special needs children, specifically autistic children. These children are locked in a kind of mental prison. It is my belief that I have the patience and imaginative thinking that can aid and improve their difficult to understand worlds.

In conclusion, I was able to put everything that I learned to a real-world experience, as a student I interned in classes ranging from kindergarten to fifth grade. During this time, I watched and listened to the students. This helped me to pinpoint exactly how they learned and to adjust my teaching style to their psychological thinking. I have also been given offered a position in a Montessori school.

In a teaching setting, good critical thinking skills are a continuous, multilayered event, where the teacher, through clarity and devotion should strive to elevate a student's sense of higher purpose (through education). The Montessori Method is a teaching system based on among other things on, individual learning and low pressure academics. "Montessori educational practice helps children develop creativity, problem solving, critical thinking and time-management skills, to contribute to society and the environment, and to become fulfilled persons in their particular time and place on earth" (Stephenson, 2009). These tenets have massive personal appeal to me and that Montessori consists of a low-stimulation environment means that I will also be working with special needs children. This path has been the fruition of a dream and a spoke in the wheel of self-actualization.

References

Decision Making Solutions. (2011).*More decision making quotes*.

Retrieved April 25, 2011, from http://www.decision making-

solutions.com/decision_making_quotes.html

Paul, R., & Elder, L. (2001). A Miniature Guide for Students on How to

Study & Learn a Discipline using critical thinking concepts & tools.

[University of Phoenix Custom Edition e-text].

Kurland, D. (2000*). What is Critical Thinking*? Retrieved April 25, 2011,

from http://www.criticalreading.com/critical_thinking.htm

Stephenson, S. (2009*). Montessori. The Montessori* Index. Retrieved April

25, 2011, from http://www.montessori.edu/index.html

A Short Story.

Army Chicken

Mason Anthony Scott

© 12/23/2014

It is said that an army travels on its stomach; no truer words were ever spoken. But a staple of every army that has ever existed has been chicken. This majestic bird has given the world so much, the feathers are used to fill beds, the eggs for breakfast and if one is so inclined, the innards can be used to catch crabs from the ocean. Trust me; you will want the crab meat after six months of chicken.

I grew up in the Deep South where the cooking of chicken was a source of pride and every family had its trade secret passed from generation to generation. It was a treat that was eaten on Sundays and then served again on Mondays. This routine was a regular the days of the week themselves. I loved it because my mother's chicken was fried deep and long giving it a crunchy taste on the outside and a juicy taste in the middle. When I joined the U.S. Army and discovered that chicken was served on a daily, I thought that I had hit the jackpot, but later and to my dismay, I had hit a jackpot that never stopped giving, the thrill were off. My heart sank; my Sunday love was now my everyday irritation.

Some nights I would have strange dreams of being pursued by Colonel Sanders riding a huge chicken that smelled of seven herbs and spices. Waking up one night after an especially horrible dream of battered and deep friend something occurred to me,

"Where does the army get all of this chicken?" and "Why do they look so mutant and huge?" The next day the mystery deepened when I asked the cook, "Where does all this chicken come from?" The look I received is the one a person gets when they ask for another person's PIN number. The cook backed away slowly and walked over to an NCO; he motioned in my direction with his head and then muttered something that caused the NCO take down my name, rank and favorite side dishes.

After this moment I was followed often around the base by men driving a black car and wearing red uniforms and white hats emblazed with the KFC logo. I needed to take my investigation deep underground and with the invention of the personal computer and something called a "library" I was able to research in peace.

One layer of the investigation lead to another, each more cryptic and hard to believe than the other but from what everybody said, I could believe everything I saw and read on the internet, I mean why would they lie and then snicker as they walked away.

What I read on a website called Wikipedia, both shocked and amazed me. The first picture showed a Tyson processing plant with a single building marked with a black X. Here the author wrote is the building where, scientists work day and night for the Pentagon, breeding and crossbreeding chickens that can withstand a nuclear, biological and chemical attack plus remain tasty. These mutant breeds are then taken to secret coops and encouraged to reproduce repeatedly by playing the soul music of Barry White.

The author then wrote about how when the chickens grow to the size of an ostrich they are taken to another secret plant located deep in the Mojave Desert and underground.

The chickens are then processed by mole people and stored for decades in the sub terrain for decades until they are delivered by a train that only goes from the Mojave to Fort Hood, Texas, then hauled by eighteen wheeler to various ports and bases around the world.

Each box that is delivered comes with special instructions to freeze until needed and cook fully. This is where my own special conspiracy comes into play, I believe that if left unfrozen the mutant chickens will thaw, come to life and began to consume the flesh of those that would consume theirs, and you've probably seen the movie. Also if not fully cooked the strange genes of the mutant chickens will cause soldiers to crow at sunrise and feed only on corn and bugs, this would be disaster because the PX will not sell either of these no matter how much you ask.

I have been out of the Army for nearly 10 years but I still wake up in a cold chill, I am seeing a VA psychologist and we are working toward my accepting chicken, he told me to start with Mc Nuggets and work my way up to a drum stick. I am making progress, I can now sit in a room with a Lemon Pepper Chicken Plug In without sweating and screaming, "Leave me alone Colonel, leave me alone".

Not a Ghost Story but a Story about a Ghost

The Faxsom Ghost

© 12/23/14

Mason Scott

Part 1

Henry Faxsom was not perplexed but pissed, he could do the math,

the boy was one years old but he had been gone for two years. The little

boy, standing there smiling and happy to see his father, was not his blood

son. His wife, the one he called lovely and loyal had never mentioned this

boy in any of her letters, never mentioned that she had been loved by

another, never mentioned that she was to be a mother and the father

was his brother.

She was ashamed but told him that the boy was not to be blamed.

The result of war ration and heated passion. "Look at me," she said, "do

not judge. This one time you will have to budge. Accept him as your son,

don't make him feel like less than none."

Faxsom wandered in his mind, from Italy to France he had left his

kind. They were lonely and so was he, it was a I need you and you need me. He supposed that were ten to twenty that were his own, that would be told that your father is unknown.

She went on to lessen the strife, "Your brother is gone, dusted from this life. Caught in the arms of the wrong man's wife. He is dead now, cold in the ground. We need not ever again see his face, we can forget this disgrace."

Henry tried for 5 years to make a connection but was never able to give affection. His mood was tolerant and bland, never giving the boy a gentle hand. "Play with me daddy," said the lad, but Henry just stared at him sad.

Five years and almost every night, Henry and his wife would fight, make love and hope for a new life from her womb but inside she was dead as a tomb.

One bright day he gave up hope and to the cellar he went with a rope. He made it short and he made it tight, this was his last action, he wanted to get it right. Jump, snap and crack, there would be no looking back. Twitching, hanging, dangling he waited for the ground to open and swell, he was going to meet his brother in hell.

He hung there and nothing was felt, he hung there like a fresh pelt. He could feel no heart beat but he felt dread, no looking back, he was dead. He sensed a movement coming from up top, a cry and a stop. "God no, not on this day, not this way!" The boy had won a contest, he wrote about his father and how he was the best. With paper in hand the boy cried loud, "No papa I wanted to make you proud."

The wake was lovely, it was nice but every dish brought was made of rice. The boy sat a window looking to the sun, his face moist with a fresh tear run. His thought was how he was to blame and that one day he might do the same.

Others talked about how Henry was always depressed, "Did you see how he dressed?" Henrys wife sat with nerves all a tatter, could not understand why he let it matter. She was the only one with a clue as to why he was so blue. Henry just stood and waited for a bell, maybe a signal from heaven or hell. He tried to leave the house and go outside but when he touched the knob it grew too wide. Now resigned to a fate worse than death, he regretted wasting his last breath.

Part Two

Mary Faxsom never remarried, she had loved with all her heart and there was nothing left for another man. Every year on the day of his death, she visited him, asking him, "Why Henry? Was your love for me so weak that you couldn't love me for whatever came?" And there is where she left the question. A question Henry never heard.

Henry would sense and see her return as just another day. He often times try to reach out to her by embracing her whenever she came home, but she could not hear his whispers or pleas for help. He wanted her to free him this world, good or bad he wanted to move on. It was torture to watch his wife mope around the house but it pained him even more to watch the boy prosper in his odd way. He would often times bring home girls that most of society would throw stones at, geeks and freaks. Like the one who shaved one side of her head and then painted the other. Or the girl who answered questions with quotes from poets. Mary hated that one the most once saying to her, "No! I do not know for whom the bells toll."

But being dead meant that he could still be there for the boy without being the cause or the cure for his life. Whenever the boy just needed to talk he called out to Henry," Old man. You there? Well, I fell in love. Momma hates her because she does not belong, she makes her own belonging. Papa, I want to be in her belonging, I want her world. I need to tell Momma that I going to be with her no matter what and that she needs to accept it. What should I do?" Henry thought about this and he knew the girl he was talking about, the one that. This girl was especially special, she had no hair, shaved to the bone, wore deep purple eye shadow all around her eyes and wore clothes that were made from a substance that the boy's mother was positive had been declared illegal. She ate no meat, to her killing anything with a brain was like killing one of own.

Henry tried to tell him, "Of course she doesn't like her. She is from another planet! Who wants an Martian for a daughter in law?" The boy never heard this so he just assumed that his dad would be happy with his decision, after all, his father was guilty of leaving and leaving his mother grieving. The boy figured that he owed him that much.

His wife was miserable and the boy had not needed him after all. Henry realized that he could have lived a full life without a true son to call his own. He could have joined a club that wore antlers on their heads and rubbed cow shit on their noses. Yes, henry thought, I really missed out on all that life had to offer.

Outside his window every day, just to make matters worse and him wonder, an odd sight happened, a cow would explode and a rainbow would flow from carcass. This was torture in itself. No man should have to mark time with a rupturing, rainbow spewing cow.

One day the view inside began to change, "Well dad, Marka and I getting married. She promised Momma she would let her hair grow out but she drew the line at the eye shadow. I am starting a new life with my future wife. I want Momma to sell the house so we can all move forward and live a place where we can go into a cellar." Even Henry would not go into the cellar. But to leave? What would be left? This shell of wood and roaches to keep him company. "No!" he screamed, "at least leave your mother! Don't leave me alone, I need you!" Henry heard himself say this, another regret to live with eternally.

When the boy told his mother Henry tried to interfere with his whispers, "Mary, the boy has lost his mind. That girl is patient zero and she will give him the weirdo's!" Mary replied to her son," I am tired of this drafty house. Every time I come in I feel a cold draft greet me."

Henry went into a fit. The door to the cellar flew open, a gust blew a smell and a sound that could only be described as hate concentrated. "See what you made me do Mary! See what happens when you don't give shit about how I feel! Stay Mary please!" Henry screamed. Mary sat frozen, horror and tears in her eyes told Henry that he gave her the final push out of his life.

The last day of the last time she closed the door Mary said, "I love you Henry."

Part Three

The seasons past and nothing last and on the third season of nothing the door knob clicked. Till this time the roaches and the rats kept Henry company, the rats ate the roaches and roaches ate the rats. The family that Henry saw walk in made him stare deep and beg to God, "Not this dear Lord! More Martians." The man's hair was longer than his wife's and hers was colored green. The man wore pants that were faded and torn, the wife wore pants but a skirt over them. The son, the son looked like he was allowed to dress himself and only wash when the moon was full and he came off a fresh kill.

The realtor mentioned something that Tanya Heal already knew. The reason the house had sat empty so long was Henry Faxsom and his cellar 'incident." Nobody in town wanted a house where a man had given up and decided to chicken out. There wasn't a soul in town who didn't know the horror of Henry.

Henry watching from the corner wanted company but not this collection of freaks and sewage leaks. The woman only spent half a minute in the kitchen and the man made sure the door from the kitchen to the garage opened and shut. The boy was out back throwing sticks hopelessly into the air at butterflies. Henry thought, that might be the only normal thing about the boy.

The realtor was having a mental shit fit, yes or no? This was the third house she had showed the family today and every house had been a house of death. The first was a grandmother that had taken her life after her husband had passed on. The second was the scene of a mass murder after a father had been laid off for the third time. What were these people looking for?

Tanya was the first to open her mouth and give the realtor relaxing words. "We'll take it.", she said and smiled at her husband Sam. The Heals were ready to settle down as a family after two years of playing every shithole from the east to the west and the north to the south. The Heals music was rock interpretive, in other words they took popular music and twisted it by playing it the complete opposite of what it was meant to be. The Heals son would dress up and dance, passing around a rainbow straw hat for coins and cash. This made Sam a little uncomfortable but they needed the money.

Sam Heal was happy to be in a place where he felt that there was still hope for his son. He realized the boy could not read when a woman in Denny's shrieked and screamed at him to "get out of the ladies room." The next piece of the puzzle was at a Wal-Mart in Dallas. When told to go and get a pair of underwear in his size he came back with a pack of 3 petite panties. Sam laughed and said, "No son, wrong bag. You know, what you wear under your pants." After several minutes, he came back with a medium pair, same bag different size. Sam then realized that it was not because he could not read the bag, it was what he preferred. He took

Buck over to the boys section and showed him the bag he needed. Buck

looked confused and said, "These have lace."

Tanya Heal was not happy about leaving the road, her life had been

about being the next Janis Joplin. But in tears, she accepted the fact that

Buck was worth a fuck.

Tanya wondered if the rope that the dead man used to hang himself

was still in place. "May I see the basement", she asked. "Oh yes, right this

way. Watch your step. The place is not insured and if you hurt yourself,

well, you hurt yourself." What a cunt, thought Tanya.

As they descended the steps the realtor was feeling the thrilling. If

one little suicide did not bother the weird woman then this place was sold

and she could put the commission towards her husband's bail and his 10

inch penis.

Henry, having been amused by Bucks dog barking at him had not

seen the basement door open until was too late, "No!", he tried to

scream. The basement was place of pain, his point of purgatory. Buck Heal

ran down first, followed gleefully by the realtor, the Sam and Tanya.

"Where did off himself", asked Sam, Tanya elbowed him for that question. The realtor led them over to the beam that was imprinted with barely noticeable notches to the naked eyes. Sam had to flick his Bic and squint his eyes just to see imagine a groove. Tanya ran her fingers slowly over the groove, feeling the direction the rope cut as the life of Henry Faxsom was squeezed out.

The basement was cold, dull and spooky. It was perfect for contacting the other world and its billions of inhabitants, good and bad. This insane idea had come upon her in New Orleans while playing a Bourbon Street club named the Old Fellow Club. The owners of the lowest bar on the lowest side invited them for drinks after closing. The owner's wife was notorious for her love of the dead, "They miss us and we envy them", she would say. After getting to know Sam and Tanya she comfortable bringing out her silk covered, mahogany Ouija board.

Sam thought it was hokey but Tanya's eyes lit up like a dying star. As they sat around a table built only for four, Sam, Tanya, Frisco the bar owner and his blind, albino wife Barb held their fingers on the wooden triangle as Barb called out for her dead uncle Andre. "Uncle Andre, where are you? Come to see me. I have a question or two for you."

Scentless air, dull light, windows still, warm skin and bowels quiet, the room was dead. Musk, bright light, window rattle, cool skin and bowels quaked, "Uncle Andre is that you?" Barb asked. Fingers itched and towards "yes". Tanya and Sam, sweat dripping from their genitals were warned not to remove their fingers from the wooden triangle, "Bring spirits from the other side, and give them a ride." Barb brought Sam and Tanya into the circle asking, "Sam and Tanya, is their somebody you know done passed on? Somebody dead and long gone." Tanya, giddy but guarded did know a soul she wanted to talk to, her father, Big Rollin' Jim. Big Rollin' Jim muled herion for the highest bidder for 20 years. Not a man that believed in bank accounts, he hid his money in deserted homes all across the country.

www.ingramcontent.com/pod-product-compliance
Lightning Source LLC
Chambersburg PA
CBHW062020280526
45787CB00005B/2180